AMERICAN MYTHOLOGY

AMERICAN MYTHOLOGY

Raphael Kosek

Brick Road Poetry Press
www.brickroadpoetrypress.com

Kateri and Stan

Cover art: "American Progress" (1872) by John Gast

Author photo: © Kateri Kosek

Library of Congress Control Number: 2019947475
ISBN: 978-0-9979559-9-6

Published by Brick Road Poetry Press
513 Broadway
Columbus, GA 31902-0751
www.brickroadpoetrypress.com

Brick Road logo by Dwight New

Table of Contents

I.

Red Canna, 1924..5
Wild West Dirge..6
Samurai Sword..8
Dorothy Bradford..9
Holding Terror..11
Through the Window of the Valley Medical Building
    in January..13
Pilgrims..15
Mary Todd Lincoln..16
Letting Go..18
November's War..19
Twenty-One Days..20
Common Mercies..21
Revolution on a Cloudy Day..22
April's Kitchen..23
The Way West..25
Wash Day..27
Sunflower, New Mexico, II, 1935..29
Heat and Snow..30
Flood..31

II.

From the Plains 1, 1919..35
Weather Forecast..36
The Lost America of Love..38
Prophet..39
Crows..40
The Day Before..41
Epoch of Anger..42
Ars Poetica..43
A Wife for the Twenty First Century (Newly Defined)..45
Stump in Red Hills, 1940..47
New World Triptych: *Raven in Red*..48
    Red Raven 1: Baptism..48
    Red Raven 2: November..49
    Red Raven 3: Learning Winter..50

Landscape sans Christina..52
Not the Thing..54
Greening..56
Seascape with Salt Marsh..58
From the Plains 1, 1953..59
Always the River: A Novel (abridged).......................................60

III.

Pelvis with Moon, 1943..65
American Mythology...66
At the Rodeo, New Mexico, 1929...68
Journey with Man and Crows..69
Wild..70
White Flower on Red Earth, 1943...71
What Matters..72
Buffalo..73
On the Suicide of Meriwether Lewis..74
Antelope, 1954..76
Young Man Lighting Up...77
Swimming with Horses...79
The Glitter Bird..80
Black Place No. 2, 1944..82

Acknowledgments..85
About the Author...86

"The essential American soul is hard, isolate, stoic, and a killer. It has never yet melted . . . The most unfree souls go west, and shout of freedom."

—D. H. Lawrence, *Studies in Classic American Literature*

I.

"The sun so hot I froze to death."

—Stephen Foster, *Oh Susanna!*

Red Canna, 1924

Georgia O'Keeffe

You are not a flower but a firestorm,
nothing hotter than your reds and yellows,
the purple bleed of your exploding heart,
grief offered up gold as joy.

You are the hoped for Mardi Gras,
the Friday night of the soul.
Anyone who burrows into your lips,
the crackle of your flame,

anyone who wakes and wakes
in the stirring sheaves of your heart,
does not go home again.

Wild West Dirge

"Shoot me," she said,
    "before they come over the hill."
With her last whiskey breath she said,
    "Nice guitar!"
In fact she had gotten caught
    in the strings of his guitar
just as she had always wished
    and the notes were
food and love and everything
    with many *o* sounds
the way mournful was beautiful
    and tears were cowboys
crying down her cheeks
    and America was no kind
of song but every major chord
    gone minor
with blackbirds heavy
    in the branches
and freight trains lunging across
    prairies silent with snow.

Such a stunning funeral! She was
    waked by buffalo
and little Annie Oakley's ghost
    grown thick in the waist,
but her trigger finger shone silver
    in the light of the corn moon
hung down from heaven,
    and some cowboy's horse
nickered in the dry streambed

when they found her body—
the rose of her mouth
    amen-ing such a gospel
the Lord couldn't ignore.

Samurai Sword

. . . a man was swinging a samurai sword
and I don't know if it came to me in the sludge
of sleep or the voice on the radio while the coffee
steamed and hissed but a man was swinging
a samurai sword while a staggered V of geese
fluted above me as I stepped out into the new day
with all the old anxieties, buttoning every button
against the wind while leaves tore round my feet
and the secret tide of salt pressed upstream
towards Albany in the great river grey and stoic
where it could go no more but return to the sea
and I understood that something would be pierced
because that is what happens when a man is swinging
a samurai sword but I didn't know what or who and when
but the river keeps flowing and the geese call
and the sun flames on the river like hot golden money
        spending itself on the last day.

Dorothy Bradford

Drowned in Provincetown Harbor December 7, 1620

With the ballast, timber and beam
    of the Old World unsteadily
beneath her, from the raw December deck
    she watches the wave chop
as though it might suddenly reveal
    an answer. She resists

studying the bleak shore bristling
    with scrub pine, barren dunes.
William has assured her it is promising
    and has gone with the rest of the men
in a shallop to reconnoiter a welcoming
    location for the saints to settle.

Unsettled, she shivers
    unable to smother images
of the young son left behind in Holland
    where the waterways are tame—
not the stormy welter of the North Atlantic,
    this world where free means

cold and blank and uninhabitable, where
    each move, each breath calls
for saintly effort beyond anything
    she can imagine.
Pay him no mind. The strangers
    grumble mutinously

and she wonders if he will find
    a sturdier wife to replace her,
for just at that moment a gull's

hacking cry splits the air—
her cue to spill herself quietly
    over the side

where the waters do not hesitate
    to welcome her.

Holding Terror

down. I am always just
    holding terror
down. What if she . . . What if
he . . . doesn't mean what
she . . . What if two, or more,
    collide?
    If the surgeon
slips, or the last step
gives way. . . if the child
wandering the woods has
    no bread crumbs
        nothing
like it? What if
    I cannot bear
morning's fingers
    prying open the day
or night's full moon
whitewashing my bedroom
    white pages
turning, turning into
the winking, yawning
round earth disengaging
    from the universe
spinning away into falling
    like falling in dreams
where we never feel
    the bottom (waking
first) but now I shall know
that jettison, the way truth
    bends metal, riddles

the windshield
while the wheel
    comes off
in my hands, roadless
    the sea
rolling in
    restless, kelp-brimmed.

Through the Window of the Valley Medical Building in January

Days of cold green rooms, old
        magazines, terse instructions,
the winter sky through slatted
        windows.
As you wait, shifting positions
        on crackling white paper,
seagulls standing in pooled water
        in parking lots
are so much better to gaze at
        than bright posters
of pink and lurid body parts
        tacked up with good intent.

Take a deep breath and hold it.

        Outside of sealed windows
trees bristle on the January mountain,
        crows caw soundlessly
where Fenimore Cooper once sent
his trackers with leather leggings,
Indian scouts, trotting down
        these steep slopes
exhaling fine and frosty breath
like smoke—their eyes
        hungry, wary.

There is no cure for this life.
Look at the seagulls, their patient huddle,
        wait-it-out attitude
while the faraway ocean

tumbles over itself
and the mountain retires into
    the dovecote of clouds.

When did evening come
without you noticing—its cool
    hand on your shoulder
making some necessary adjustment?

Pilgrims

A dog barks in solitary
obligation to the night

Shifting in their stalls,
cattle exhale sweet breath

Hills slip into morning
rising out of mists that linger,
reluctant for day's clarity

The sun's light is deflected, still,
to a feather pale moon
that dissipates into the milk sky

and earth heaves into morning,
afternoon, evening,

following the slap of tides,
the lunge of beast to its burden

and yearnings of men
who can recall no other home,
yet feel forever strange and amazed
here,

as if they had just stepped
off a ship from some far place
into the pitch and pith of this earth:

its birdsong—delirious,
its losses—stunning

Mary Todd Lincoln

I don't know how he lived with her,
she, with him. The sweet round face
bred to be happy, a full, pleasant life—
not the deep worry of a tall, thin man
who was friend to insomnia,
who weighed the light and the dark,
who deviled himself with the broken country.

How could they not drink the water
of the Potomac, lose a son
to the malaria tainted airs of a city
surrounded by swamp?—
the unspeakable sacrifice Abraham nearly made,
more real than any happiness
they ever knew, old hands at losing sons.

How to leave such losses, cut short mourning,
carry the weight?—serious responsibility
must consecrate such a one as he,
but she, with her soft full body,
her smiling into occasional madness,

some said, childishness, the spendthrift ways
as if three hundred pairs of lace gloves
could buy back what grief swallowed,
a vase here, a rich cushion there,
to soften the bare walls,
the rough hewn face that bore the brunt.

She couldn't bear to attend the funeral.

How could she not be forgiven?
Even falling into debt can have its blessings.
And madness, after all, is a haven of sorts
not far from heaven.

Letting Go

I am finally free
    of the dress,
the shoe,
    desire for
the water in the glass,
    sunny day.
No longer do I fear
the hours of the clock,
    protocol
of disappointment,
    the awful goodness
of good intentions.

I have learned how movement
is to be still,
    how hunger
is a form of divinity,
and mystery,
    the slow sifting
of one world into another.

Truth comes unexpected—
    black wings in blue sky,
    the cold, kissing moon.

Never what you think.

November's War

The wind heaves a length
of cream-colored butcher's paper
across the yard nearly
big enough to bag a body.

The leaves have been torn
from the trees and after
a pointless but violent skirmish,
a pile wells up at my back door
more than adequate
to cushion a fall.

Yes, I have prayed
but the wind sweeps
everything away until

the lawn is empty,
November's sky scoured
of any soft notion of kindness
or mercy.

At sundown tarnished clouds
gather like commanders.
The night—one big powwow,
and morning—anybody's call.

Twenty-One Days

for Catherine, mother of a soldier

Twenty-one days until he comes home
and each one fires likes the desert sun.
Her heart has long worn camouflage,
laced up the boots of its beating—
her breath tightly controlled.

She knows he will come home
different. Twenty-one pearls
on a string, she prays the cord will hold,
she curses the ties that bind.

Twenty-one eggs in a basket,
twenty-one loaves and fishes,
but if the multiplication fails . . .
Her heart wears a helmet,
her voice fills with sand.

Twenty-one miracles nearly too much
to ask. Twenty-one blackbirds
breaking out of a pie. Twenty-one reasons
not to die. No one can know

what walls have come down,
what limbs she has severed—
how she blows herself up every day.

Common Mercies

"So little do we prize common mercies when we have them to the full."
—from *The Narrative of the Captivity and Restoration of Mrs. Mary Rowlandson, 1676*

You should be so grateful
for the smooth sheets,
   quiet slide
into sleep, haloed tree
outside your window.
   Grateful
for the dull day where
no glass shatters, no voice
is raised, where you can
   wander room to room,
let the unimportant minutes tick by
   unnoticed. Grateful
for the bread, full and soft
   in your mouth,
and for your children—
   smarter, quicker, better
than you—ringing
   like the sure bell
we are all supposed to be.

Because you *know*
what can happen:
   Fire blooms,
   the curtain, torn,
   the face, hardened.
A red man at the window.

Revolution on a Cloudy Day

Pink-faced men sit around a table
where wine glows amber, and a droplet
pools on burnished wood.

Pens scratch as the wind rises
outside, and two crows circumscribe
a white sky in careless flight.

What kindles amidst earnest voices
can and cannot be heard by someone
who stands outside the door. Casual, alert.

In the shadowy room candles
flicker and fall almost like music
while the perimeters of what is possible

are pushed way past
what is safe, what is acceptable,
what can't be done.

April's Kitchen

Why do I think of Sylvia Plath
while washing parsley at the sink,
looking out the window at how fast
spring has come upon us,
the sun so strong and warm?

My son is outside chopping wood
that will weather for next winter,
the dull thunk of the axe, comforting,
the dogwood on the verge
of blossoming. He will go out
after supper, he tells me,
to see his girlfriend. I worry
they are, perhaps, too serious,
too young. I wonder what movie
they will see, what life they will make.

Then I think of Sylvia
taping the doors and windows
before she turned on the oven.
Was she wearing an apron?
Had she set her hair the night
before? Didn't she kiss
the children, one by one?

Isn't everything we do serious?
The French take their food
as a serious pleasure. I am slow
chopping the fragrant parsley,
aware the faucet is dripping
and will not stop.

I hear the thud of the axe,
watch as the wood splits cleanly,
falling to the ground
as if it knew its duty.

Drop by drop the water slips,
away and down. Stroke by stroke
destruction has a rhythm.
There is no stopping the burgeoning blooms,
the plans dark and deep,
the murderous beauty of bright things.

The Way West

My daughter is driving
    across the continent, eating cheddar
in Wisconsin, waking to a cougar's yellow
    rasp, sleeping tentless
in a corn field where a mysterious

insect leaves a sore story of welts
    over her face, her neck—
she is off my radar, and it feels like
    part of me is floating off the map,
past the flannel of sleep, the safety

of novels—I hear the wind over her phone,
    constant. The wind, her voice
informs me, never stops blowing in South Dakota
    where the Black Hills are not really black
but green and grey like Cezanne's mountains.

Her hair glistens with a mid-American
    sweat I have never felt, her car
runs into the different hours
    of a different night. We have
lost the clock between us, the familiar

gone strange. Prairie, so flat, she says,
    you can see the sun for a long time.
I feel something flatten out between us—
    and ease into a rhythm where the plains
of her life, of mine, drift

buoyant, open, rising without words,
   hours, or habits—
      new country.

Wash Day

The day is all here
hanging on the line with the laundry—
your grey shirt next to my blue one,
    the sky flying overhead
with bits of cloud like torn sleeves,
    pulled thread.

We do not speak.
    There is no wind.
What could be said
    so deep into summer?

The first tomato is pushing scarlet,
small green cucumbers curl in secret
    around wire mesh, eager
for the burgeoning future.

    Though silent,
we are the bright burning roses
    of ourselves,
heavy in yellow light.

Waters twist at our feet,
flocks of birds sweep the sky,
    and something races
through the grass
    until
heady with this life,
    blowzy, disheveled,
we come home
    like lightning,

like dust.

Like laundry.

Sunflower, New Mexico, II, 1935

Georgia O'Keeffe

You stand up fearless
in a sky so avid blue.

You think we don't have the simple heart
to rise up, knock our heavy heads

against Heaven, eat the sun
until our hair flames golden,

to kiss and wave in a never ending July.
Some of us do, but the weight

of all this wonder grows like a stone
and the sharp lace of early frost

sprouts a fine, low withering
that is not without its own grace.

Heat and Snow

After the raised voices, silence
floods in quick and clean.

I marvel at its silvery presence,
unobtrusive as water

and how, like water, it mends
the spilled savagery in the pale light

of late afternoon. The day moves
inexorably towards supper.

Words will find us later,
words about needing milk

or ironing the blue shirt and Oh yes
you found the missing button,

could I sew it on. I could.
Doubt about this life

accrues gently like snow
weighting a pine bough with a beauty

so soft, no one suspects the snap,
the weight that cannot be borne.

Flood

How hopeless it all seems late at night.
Keep it up for the children, the husband, the dog.
Don't let them see the trouble
inside you, how the white pill of the moon
is your drug of choice, how your sweaty breasts
lie heavy, awkward
after all these years against the flesh
above the ribs—
how your life abrades you.
Read a book, write a poem, go to church.
Keep your finger in the hole
for you know the flood will come,
uprooting trees, pulling up the years
like carrots.

You're tired of constructing the ark,
of safety nets, insurance.
You have never left your life,
now something in you welcomes
the restless slap of water
where it laps the dark shore,
the whining wind,
careless stranger who loiters,
horse saddled up.

II.

"It rained so hard the day I left, the weather it was dry."

—*Oh Susanna!*

From the Plains 1, 1919

Georgia O'Keeffe

When you settled in west Texas
you saw the light over the plains
like a great overturned bowl—
the sky ragged with wind
that blew for days.

The blue-green sea of light bellowed
and broke as the dark came down
as the earth thrust itself back into sky
and clouds jutted over the huge bowl
like cattle before a storm

trampling the waving grasses,
knitting down the patterned earth
while the mind raced
and the heart beat
and the wind came
like your own wild breath.

Weather Forecast

on the crash of JFK Junior's Piper Saratoga, July 16 '99 during a drought
in the Northeast

The forecast calls for diminished visibility,
but when have we ever seen clearly?
There is a chance of rain. The soil
is parched and leaves dance down
untimely in July.
　　　Only a chance,
but there are mists over the water,
risks we have to take.

They were late in taking off.
Aren't we all?
He was reluctant to fly
　　　into the night,
but let himself go into the grey
wash of evening. After all,
how many twilights have rekindled
lullabies, the float of the child
into sleep? islands vague
and beckoning?

The sharp descent, bright speed
of destruction, was nothing more
than the breath-catching nightmare
we've all ridden out of sleep.

Planes buzz overhead, men serious
in uniform, equipment even more serious,
divers divvying up the waters,
sifting the currents. Even as
they are found, can it put us right?

satisfy longing?

The seas are expected to remain
eloquent in their silence, monotonous
as they slap the hull into rocking.
Winds will delicately brush
the beach grass
*   as a mother's hand*
smoothes her child's brow
before sleep.

The Lost America of Love

from Ginsberg's "Supermarket in California"

Such comfort
    in the twang of his guitar
where I have lost myself in the strum
    that travels me down
stream, heaven of song blue wide and deep
        on a sweet green sea—
you are my very own boy, my very own
time, my high, my guy, my gypsy scarf,
        my trip good-bye.

You kick me across
    the floor of my life, spill
    my pockets, unclench my hands
till I don't know anything
        but ride this wave
    let pieces go
one by one
    down river
        down high
Don't make me give back these words,
    these notes spooling
        on your thread
your crumb of bread, just let me sing
    this breath this night pulled
        down like a drug
where I'm saved by the progression
    of your chords, your strophes,
and isn't such faith
    what everyone wants—God help us
        it's all we got.

Prophet

I'm falling through, saving up,
    drowning down. I can't
holler hopeful anymore, I drink
    dreams, magnify minutiae.
I'm sinning in songs for all those
    who cannot ignore eternity,
for all who are digging discernible
    graves. I'm shoring up
against your gravitas. Comedians
    are the saddest people I know.

    Dorothea Lange said, "Art is
an act of total attention." Snap. Click. You
    got it. You're looking at it.
I will love you if you let me. Leave
    the mirror, turn the page. Words
are crackers that crumble.
    We're expecting a monster
storm. The trees stand up and whistle
    and the sky, she rains.
Ease into your skin, pile the sandbags,
    the war's not over.
We are the war.

Crows

To get over their darkness,
        their funereal feathers,
the stark calligraphy of their flight,
        I have made crows my friends,
loving them as my own,
accepting their watchful eye,
    watching them prance
as they eat my bread.

I believe in what they preach
    rising up before me,
beating the air with blackened wings,

these messengers of constant mourning,
    friends of the casual corpse,
announcing apostasy,

warning us of what we have already
    learned here—
that their blackness is nothing
    next to ours.

The Day Before

the Fourth of July
    we dutifully hang
the now faded military flag
awarded my uncle at his death,
and somehow this year
we leave it out longer by
    mutual but silent
agreement that we need
    its fitful fluttering
 in the damp wind the week after
 the Fourth as storms gather
    sullen and heavy each day
and the old belief that everything
will right itself
    no longer holds
as the radio spits news at us
and the twilight barely placates
    a longing for
this sweet bird of youth,
our rumpled darling
     July 2016

Epoch of Anger

A little man with a big dog
    and an American flag
emblazoned on his jacket
    stopped my friend's daughter
while she was walking in Manhattan:
    "Immigrant, go back where
you belong!"
    Her daughter is tall
and olive skinned and she kept
    walking, but the flare
of the little man's anger was
    hard like a pellet gun
and she felt the bruise on her skin,
    saw the dog's hair bristle,
smelled its clouded slobber long after
    they had passed.

Ars Poetica

I want to write the poem
    that will break your window,
tear your pants, the poem
    that won't stop bleeding
and scares you serious.

My poem will
    swallow a toad,
pluck feathers from blackbirds,
reek of the bear's den
    and onions on your knife.
It will go blue in the face
    and do badly on tests.
It drinks too much
    and doesn't know
when to leave, starts fires
    and twirls tornadoes.

My poem was a dust bowl
    and a sky beating with
        passenger pigeons,
a swale where bodies were pulled
    from the mud of millennia.
Now it's kudzu and bindweed
    and bent on
        blackening the world.
It's a splinter that troubles
    your flesh, enters foreign
and clean. You don't know
my poem is in you
        until it festers

and agitates, fevers
and sweats you and by then
    it's too late.

A Wife for the Twenty First Century (Newly Defined)

I am the wife of the fork
and the spoon and the knife,
of the bowls rattling in their cupboard,
of the howling of the house.

I am the wife of the velvet muzzled dog,
the delicate cat, of the lilacs bowing
outside the window, of the moon—
sleepless white eye of the night.

I am the wife of the bad dream,
the sweating and falling, the shoe
and the slipper, of the traffic
and the rain, of church on Sunday,

and the sea in July. I am the wife
of those who let themselves go,
who reach for the bottle, the hammer,
—small angry god of war.

I am the wife of the fly and the gnat that
cluster and shine in the eye of the dead.
Of the crow that swings down
on such carrion spread. I am the wife

of intemperate grief, the river rising,
brittle limbs bending back in a wind
all trouble, all promise, all scatter.
Black cloak of the heart—you summon

me like the blackbird's high whistle
whose call becomes the thin song
of my life. I am the wife who will weep
when the eye of the world

closes, and the last flock flaps away
tearing the drop-cloth of sky that
separates this life from the other,
the husband from the wife.

Stump in Red Hills, 1940

Georgia O'Keeffe

No matter who you are or where you go
you will find yourself in these red hills
one day—their almost lurid glow
like the plump and purpled heart itself.

See how the wood is tormented
into a shape that aches
for the tree it once was,
now only a fetal splintering, sinuous
throb of raw nerve, so intense
you cannot look

but she has opened your eyes
and you feel the twist of the trunk,
know what it is to writhe in red hills
to be heavy with desire

for that which is unseeable, unknowable,
for that which has no name
and calls to you in a thousand red voices.

New World Triptych: *Raven in Red*

Sheojuk Etidlooie, Inuit graphic

Red Raven 1: Baptism

Clouds stream eloquently
    shrouding earth. Water falls
upon water
    upon stone
        running rivulets
washing rushing cobbles, pebbles
    clattering. Red raven
watches from his tree—
    calling down a hundred
silences upon us, shattering air with
    his beak, his vowel, his gospel—
hurt silence to bring us
    to our senses, to drown us
in such leaf such branch, the clear flood
    of sky, each page each wave
each bursting blossom
    crushed to the heart:

    this is what it means
to live in our skins, to roam
    the hills of this body this blue
        this bread we eat
we breathe until wings cover us
    dun and dove, oyster and sand
so good to die forever
    in mornings that rise
from mists settling,
        settling.

Red Raven 2: November

opens its bare limbed sky above us
    waves its last crimson or gold head—
its sun, the last grace or mercy
      before winter sinks its tooth
        deep.

Sunset bleeds rose into mercury
    into pewter
      that begs the question

why does your beauty hurt—
    the heart-shaped leaf, red fox
      disappearing into dark wood,
hawk's high cry piercing the air
    like flesh?

Our faith makes us shiver,
    each day we scan the sky—
      simpletons—
teach us, show us, reveal yourself
    where the wind turns the leaves
      and a grace note of moon hangs
among chary clouds.
      No sign of Red Raven.

What bitter and fragrant grass
    have we not yet tasted?

Which beauty will be the final one?

Red Raven 3: Learning Winter

Before snow
the air tastes metal
under a cathedral sky
where we go down on our knees
to medieval winter,
and pray hard
to basilicas of ice,
conifers that writhe
and twist like Bernini's columns
connecting earth to heaven.

First, we learn winter
as a form of meditation,
then a difficult litany. Winter
is everything
we cannot imagine:
what it is like to kneel
on stone
to shudder in the thin garment
of our faith
barely covering in the cold,
to suffer the hovel, the mind, the earth
so dark
for so long
the stone unturned
the counting like waiting
like praying

until the veil of snow
transforms the landscape
where crows congregate

in wood's silent pulpit
    where we begin
to learn everything
    we cannot know.
Red Raven is the only fire
    in winter's cold sea,
but hidden far and deep
    among dark branches
      under night
where snow falling
    is the only word, the only.

Landscape sans Christina

upon reading an old interview with Andrew Wyeth just after his death

"Lonely" my mother complains
about the paintings hanging
on my walls bereft of people:
    late winter sun
bruising the silent snow, but no
stark figure bundled against the cold.
    A river toils out to sea
where no one paddles a modest boat
or stands on the bridge to fish—only
the grass in collusion with the wind
where a dusty-eyed child might be
    dreaming summer away
but isn't. Then I wonder

could there even be
    a paradise
without Adam and Eve—
    their restless hunger, desirous
    eye, fingers entwined
in the wild green hair
    of plants, the friction
    of flesh, their trembling
when a tree falls?

Andrew Wyeth sometimes regretted
painting Christina
    into "Christina's World,"
believing that
    from the weathered grey
of the sentinel house,

the gunmetal gleam
of the ocean always
    just over the rise,
field inclining upwards to meet
    the paled sky,
we should *feel* her presence

yearning in that sea of grass
endlessly grounded, her lovely
    and crippled
body, redundant, after all.

Not the Thing

but the small diamond of
    expectation,
not the day but the slow
    blooming of light
before the whale of sun
    clears the horizon,
not the loon
    but its tongue
 piercing morning fog

    faint
flutter of wing
    ahead of flight,
water waiting before
    the dive, the moment after
lightning but before
    thunder. Not the word
but what sets it afloat,
    not the puzzle
but the curiosity,
    not the question

but the sea of vagary
        that spawns
not love, no, but your
    fingers grazing
the arm before intention.
    Not death, but the living
        multitudinous

that leads to it.
    Not you but your
pillow, white and clean.

Greening

The crickets keep ticking away
like a current that floats me
    buoyant through the open
window while the roadbed
    flatlines with traffic,
        distant, erratic,
the night air pressing in against
    my skin, faintly moist, the lick
of a moon, all telling me time
    is manageable this way—
house quiet, the country
    of night
doesn't mind or need
    to keep tabs—only sweet air
swimming in through the window
    like some dark
        and deserved
sedative, so I give up filling
    the coffers
        of my need—
let the orphans raid my cupboards,
let the drivers hurtle towards
    neon love,
let the black greening of June night swell
        my heart.
    Done drinking precious
tides—I minister to the fallen—
    I am one who falls
knee-deep in night, the wild choke

of spring dew, damp moon
cooling the skies—no place to go
but up.

Seascape with Salt Marsh

When I close my eyes in cover of trees
at the edge of salt marsh, wind
    moving through oak and pine
       sounds like rain.
How curious that wind could be water,
    one thing, another.

The smell of salt, mud flats
    when the tide goes out
recalls the body, when honest sweat
    assures us of the good animal
within, our days measured against
    the fluid drift of clouds.
Yet we cleave to our identities,
wearing them like clothes, lipsticked in,
    cinched with a belt.

    Don't you feel
the way wind runs through us, water
always pulls us,
    how bird song trills
from our throats,
       how we disappear
with the last light, waver
       with the first star?

From the Plains 1, 1953

Georgia O'Keeffe

A flat strip of umber brown earth
covered in fire red, tangerine,
the platform for the enormous flaming
sun that shoots a jagged fire
into the reddened sky,
reminds us we are children of fire,
of light that blinds.

Have we not learned to drink
this hot golden cup
until we rise and burn
growing anxious as all the sharp
and glittering stars?

Always the River: A Novel (abridged)

. . . and they paddled for days, the water
glinting hard in their eyes. Grey
is what happens to blue at twilight.

I know this is how the soul travels,
how we keep moving up river
from wherever we are—skimming past

trees in full frock, slippery banks, the blind
eyes of houses. *He says something to her*
and she says something back. Words like stones

tumbled and cool, precise or incidental. Movement
is what we have, water-spray—its blessing.
Around the next bend—catbird whistling

while moonlight's cold white money fills
our coffers. We pull the pale silver in earnest
ritual—through deceit, lust, forgiveness, the world's

wild holler—believing this is the way
as we cut the deep green dark, hungering like
the early explorers, hatless, brazen, from glory to glory.

III.

"I had a dream the other night when everything was still."

—*Oh Susanna!*

Pelvis with Moon, 1943

Georgia O'Keeffe

White angel, balustrade of bone,
the bluest piece of sky
is framed in your elegant portal
as you buttress the bone moon
on your bleached hip

where warm flesh, haunch of steer
or pony, procreational pivot
once saddled you to your spent mortality
where you breathed red dust
roamed blue mountains

where your stony eye rolled white
and wild when the man encircled you
with his rope. Such pink living,
such beaten paths so far
from the sea

and now your gleaming bone
resembles nothing so much
as a pierced and dazzling whorl
of shell with the sea of sky
leaking through, a windy
trumpet of soundless music,
a gorgeous vacancy
unbridled, no longer ridden
or driven or dreaming,
but a window to heavenly space.

American Mythology

I've never been out west
but the frontier is in my bones—
all those cowboys from childhood
churning up the dust on countless
horses—Sugarfoot, Rowdy Yates,
Maverick, and the Bonanza boys—
oh how they knew

how to be cruel
and kind—the right dose of tough,
the brilliant smile under a cocked
hat as they righted the world. Death
on camera was never real
though they spoke with guns
besting the Indians played by
mournful Mexicans

with painted faces.

I learned to keep my wagons moving
while the great horse of the world
dips and sways with currents unseen:
savor the hard edge,

feel the blade,
keep your legs tight and bend into
the wind which blows every which way
but where you figured. Sand in your

teeth, you keep crossing rivers

losing
your footing, your horse, your bearing;
crawling over the mountains you are
so high you jettison what holds you back:

that last barrel, book, word, belief,
but not the whiskey
never the whiskey. You starve
your mother, leave
                your child, this
is how you tackle

a frontier that pulls you farther and
farther away until
        you are gone
into a sky so big
    you cry for words,
fill your pockets with dirt
    and your mouth
        with stones.

There you go
    descending
into all those gaping canyons
never to return—
                heartless vagabond,
                    broken, unspeakable,
leaning into a copper wind.

At the Rodeo, New Mexico, 1929

Georgia O'Keeffe

You understand we don't all ride bulls
for a living, but the yoke-yellow eye
in the center of your garish corral
says we may as well
crack ribs in the dusty ring
of this life, ride high fliers
until the bloodshot eye
of some aggravated beast
has it in for us,

until we are welted in blue-black—
just another color of blood,
until the flesh of our dream,
the huge risk we take

is carnival pulp under
the sharp hooves
of whatever rides us

and the brutal well-meant
cries of strangers rain down
like hard chips of turquoise sky.

Journey with Man and Crows

The saw and swing of it—
    that beauty ride, that gorgeous gallop
      that whistling in the hills,
swanning on the water
    as our boats glide unwavering
      through the deep valleys
cutting color like stained glass until
    riotous rising of the pheasant
      from the soft sedge of bottomlands,
rising like the very heart itself
    in the man who looks long
      who breathes the air—incredulous
at what knocks in his chest, what
    floats over the river lifting
      to the tops of wintered trees
where the crows gather and gather
    adding their cries to his life,
      their noteless unwritten music
piercing old timber, deepening distance.

Wild

*"I expect to leave my own bones unburied, to bleach in the woods,
or to be torn asunder by the wolves."*
　　　　—Hawk-Eye in James Fenimore Cooper's *Last of the Mohicans*

I see me a beast
   tongue, tooth, sharp
talon piercing the furred blur
   running away, out of
into, down the dark hole, tunnel
   or treetops tilting above
ragged earth where the pelt
   corrodes, rotting
into forest sweet floor
   ashiver with worm
under the wolf-howled moon
   where our dreams run
dark and slippery
   gasping for breath with
fin, feather, flesh beneath
   the wagging, drooling,
bleeding, barking down
   the throat which is
what struggles to emerge
   to choke and poke
into the cavities of pinecones
   marrow of bone, the scruffy
snarl, mud-suck of secrets fertile:
   a glorious stink
something will eat
   leaning deep
     into its hunger.

White Flower on Red Earth, 1943

Georgia O'Keeffe

Perhaps the most plebeian white
of all your white flowers,
the faithful yellow eye gazes full front,
curiously flat:
>   *I am nothing*
> *but what I am, my leaves,*
> *dandelion ugly, lay close*
> *on red earth the color*
> *of dried blood, my petals*
> *open so far that little is left*
> *of me like you*

> *when you open yourself to the world,*
> *when migrating herds trammel*
> *   the grass of your hair,*
> *the lakes of your eyes brim*
> *   with red dust,*
> *and birds flame*
> *   from your famished mouth.*

What Matters

is when you thought all the hummingbirds
    had flown for the season
but you see one at the feeder
    bent on swilling enough sugar water
for the trip south. What matters

is even though you burned your toast
    while writing this down,
you realize seeing the hummer
    meant so much more
than burnt toast. What matters

is not how long we are married
    and how the years have
taught us how different we are
    but that you still call me
when you walk by the river
    on your lunch break
and the river still flows on
    silent and deep. What matters

is not that we never got that house
    near the ocean, but that its
waves lap and crash within me
    every day, and there's
a gull lifting a corner of the sky
    forever
in my peripheral vision.

Buffalo

President Obama officially designated the bison our national mammal
    May 2016

How can we live up to
    the heft of your buffalo heart
housed in the belligerent humped body?
    Your dark eyes glower as you
stand guard over what you love
    what you nurture
while the waving silvered prairie grasses
    bend in the wind acquiescing to
the willful hum of bees, the driven
    frenzy of season begetting season
until it thrums in the heart of painters

like Catlin who had to get your agony
    just right so he let you die
slowly after one bullet to record
    the "grim-visaged monster—
swelling with rage"
    in the name of art. Such a brutal
love of beauty is our trademark, and he would
    ride off each day with the tribe
on their hunts in search of true American
    flesh—then we diligently killed off
your species only to bring you back—
    a serious beast
with your hard-bitten love
    all salt and fury and shag
more real than any painting
    despite our love of symbols.

On the Suicide of Meriwether Lewis

When you could no longer
follow the silver, spinning arm
of the river to the sea,

when you could no longer count
layers of unnamed mountains
rearing up in frigid challenge

or grow dizzy as the plains
swelled with buffalo,
or sink into sleep weary with wonder
surrounded by companions equally
exhausted and incredulous,

when you were only weary
with disputations and grievances,
debts and the bone heaviness
that civilization brought
to the Louisiana Territory,

you mourned in one evening's
twilight at a small inn
on the Natchez Trace, trying
to fall asleep on a buffalo skin,
unable to reclaim the old journey

with its purpose clear
as birdcall, sharp
as the sting of buffalo dung
on the morning air.

So you sent yourself away
with a gun to the head
and a gun to the heart
nearly simultaneously,
      or so they say.

Antelope, 1954

Georgia O'Keeffe

Your pronged antlers
seem poised to spring off
of the grounded skull
with its eyeless sockets
into the salmon sky
that simmers over flat desert.

Oh heart, you leap lightly
out into this world
of blossom, of sand, of craved
and craving flesh—
you just want to live
until you die,

you want to pull cool grass,
clamber from ledge to ledge,
to close your flickering eyelids
until nothing knits you to this earth
and you fly far from its mortal economies.

Young Man Lighting Up

The young man paused
    just long enough
to cup his hand lovingly
    around the cigarette
lighting it before stepping out
into the clench of four-lane traffic
    weaving his way
among us as I watched him
    slim and confident, bent
on reaching the store across
the street, careless with the surety
of youth, and I can only assume
    he reached his destination
as I didn't hear the screech of brakes
or bray of horns as the light
    turned.
        The following
day I recalled him
    with longing,
        something connate,
and he grew
    in significance because
it was so insignificant—precisely why
I kept seeing him
    doing what we all do
        cupping our hands
around the thin flame of something
    we nurture for good or ill
as we step into the world's

thrash—confident, fully believing
   we will reach
      the other side.

Swimming with Horses

is like nothing else: the heavy body
svelte and muscled entering
the lightness of water—blue tipping plate
  of the lake, melding with
an earthy beast, a steady heart, the healthy
fear like a jet tearing
  the night sky of your bones.

"Swim!" the trail guide yells. You slip
  off the horse,
   find the water yourself,
the under-thrash of hooves, equine eye
   that corrals you like God—
hands, legs slicing the wind-chop
of water. You've never been so
  water-blind in sun, scraping

up onto the glazed stones
of the far shore, cord in your hands, finding
  your feet and breathing
hard: Hauled up, emerging
as if for the first time, the trees
  waving, the sky bright shining.

The Glitter Bird

When I saw you, oh bird, oh bird of mine
up on the highest branch of the tallest tree,
your beak curved and shining in your
blue-black towering raven's way—your
feathers all black and bundled beautiful—
oh how you took my eye with your gleaming
way—you could fly me over those bristling
mountains, over the brilliant and thrashing
sea. Oh bird, can you mend my broken
ways? Pierce the ripening globe
of the sun with the golden thrust of your
beak? Break out the hesitant moon
with the stuttering knife of your throaty
calling? You could make scarce my devils
and divulge my treasures lain low
beneath grey waters—with your talons
pull up the fat heart so that its beating
is the nursery rhyme for all to hear.
You could clearly mark the mess
of my days—crying before me
all wild and wandering children.

When I saw you, oh bird, oh mine,
you were much more than the deflated
helium balloon escaped from some
celebration of life's passage, sculpted
by wind and my capacity for wonder
swaying beyond clear vision
up on the highest branch of the tallest tree

catching the new morning light
with great intent.

Black Place No. 2, 1944

Georgia O'Keeffe

This is the place where we all crack,
the snaking fissure where lovers fall away:
the disappointed, stunned, the failed
and finished.

This is where the earth opens and we slip
into something that goes so deep
into soil, into rock, into pink-fleshed
granite

—the place where we must learn
to love our life when we have nothing,
the rock hard bed of it, grey pillow of stone.

This is where we break our teeth on beauty,
swallow silence for our daily bread.
If we dare look up, white clouds
churn in the broken blue,
and yes, the horse will find his way
home, with or without us.

Acknowledgments

Some of the poems in this manuscript, or versions of them, have appeared in two chapbooks, *Letting Go* (Finishing Line Press), and *Rough Grace* (Concrete Wolf Press), and the following journals which the author gratefully acknowledges.

Big Muddy: "On the Suicide of Meriwether Lewis"

Briar Cliff Review: "Buffalo"

Catamaran: "Pelvis with Moon"

Chattahoochee Review: "Swimming with Horses"

Common Ground Review: "Dorothy Bradford"

Comstock Review: "*At the Rodeo, New Mexico,*" "*Black Place No. 2,*" and "Letting Go"

Frost Foundation Website: "Journey with Man and Crows"

Holly Rose Review: "Holding Terror"

Hudson River Valley Review: "Through the Window of the Valley Medical Center"

Juxtaprose: "Samurai Sword"

Kalliope: "Heat and Snow"

Margie: Journal of American Poetry: "Mary Todd Lincoln"

New Millennium: "Twenty-One Days"

The Recorder: "*Red Canna*"

Pinyon: "Wild West Dirge"

Poetry East: "The Way West"

Rhino: "Crows"

Silk Road: "Landscape sans Christina"

Slant of Light: Contemporary Women of the Hudson Valley: "A Wife for the 21st Century"

Southern Humanities Review: "Always the River"

About the Author

Raphael Helena Kosek lives in and draws inspiration from the beautiful Hudson Valley where she lives with her husband and three cats. Her latest chapbook, *Rough Grace*, won the 2014 Concrete Wolf Chapbook Competition and her essay, "Meditations on the Common Life," tied for first place in the 2016 *Eastern Iowa Review*'s Lyric Essay Contest. Her poetry won first place in the *Bacopa Literary Review*'s 2019 poetry contest, where her essay "Caregiver's Journal: How to Survive or Not" won first place in 2016 and was nominated for a Pushcart Prize. She is the 2019 Dutchess County, New York Poet Laureate, and she teaches English at Marist College and Dutchess Community College where her students keep her real.

Our Mission

Brick Road

Poetry Press

www.brickroadpoetrypress.com

The mission of Brick Road Poetry Press is to publish and promote poetry that entertains, amuses, edifies, and surprises a wide audience of appreciative readers. We are not qualified to judge who deserves to be published, so we concentrate on publishing what we enjoy. Our preference is for poetry geared toward dramatizing the human experience in language rich with sensory image and metaphor, recognizing that poetry can be, at one and the same time, both familiar as the perspiration of daily labor and as outrageous as a carnival sideshow.

Available from Brick Road Poetry Press

BRICK ROAD
POETRY PRESS
www.brickroadpoetrypress.com

Just Drive by Robert Cooperman

The Alp at the End of My Street by Gary Leising

The Word in Edgewise by Sean M. Conrey

Household Inventory by Connie Jordan Green

Practice by Richard M. Berlin

A Meal Like That by Albert Garcia

Cracker Sonnets by Amy Wright

Things Seen by Joseph Stanton

Battle Sleep by Shannon Tate Jonas

Lauren Bacall Shares a Limousine by Susan J. Erickson

Ambushing Water by Danielle Hanson

Having and Keeping by David Watts

Assisted Living by Erin Murphy

Credo by Steve McDonald

The Deer's Bandanna by David Oates

Creation Story by Steven Owen Shields

Touring the Shadow Factory by Gary Stein

Also Available from Brick Road Poetry Press

www.brickroadpoetrypress.com

Dancing on the Rim by Clela Reed

Possible Crocodiles by Barry Marks

Pain Diary by Joseph D. Reich

Otherness by M. Ayodele Heath

Drunken Robins by David Oates

Damnatio Memoriae by Michael Meyerhofer

Lotus Buffet by Rupert Fike

The Melancholy MBA by Richard Donnelly

Two-Star General by Grey Held

Chosen by Toni Thomas

Etch and Blur by Jamie Thomas

Water-Rites by Ann E. Michael

Bad Behavior by Michael Steffen

Tracing the Lines by Susanna Lang

Rising to the Rim by Carol Tyx

Treading Water with God by Veronica Badowski

Rich Man's Son by Ron Self

About the Prize

BRICK ROAD
POETRY PRESS
www.brickroadpoetrypress.com

The Brick Road Poetry Prize, established in 2010, is awarded annually for the best book-length poetry manuscript. Entries are accepted August 1st through November 1st. The winner receives $1000 and publication. For details on our preferences and the complete submission guidelines, please visit our website at www.brickroadpoetrypress.com.

Winners of the Brick Road Poetry Prize

www.brickroadpoetrypress.com

2018

Speaking Parts by Beth Ruscio

2017

Touring the Shadow Factory by Gary Stein

2016

Assisted Living by Erin Murphy

2015

Lauren Bacall Shares a Limousine by Susan J. Erickson

2014

Battle Sleep by Shannon Tate Jonas

2013

Household Inventory by Connie Jordan Green

2012

The Alp at the End of My Street by Gary Leising

2011

Bad Behavior by Michael Steffen

2010

Damnatio Memoriae by Michael Meyerhofer